# GUNS N' ROSES
## THE PICTURES

## PHOTOGRAPHS BY GEORGE CHIN

**OMNIBUS PRESS**
LONDON · NEW YORK · SYDNEY

6/1/92
GN'R
World Tour
The
ALL ACCESS
Mother Blue

# INTRODUCTION

THE FIRST TIME I MET GUNS N'ROSES WAS WHEN THEY CAME TO LONDON IN JUNE 1987. IT WAS AT THE FLAT IN KENSINGTON WHERE THEY WERE STAYING. MY VERY FIRST IMPRESSION WAS THAT THEY LOOKED VERY LA, WITH THEIR COWBOY BOOTS, LEATHER JACKETS, TIGHT JEANS, LOTS OF SPURS AND JANGLY BANGLES.

OVER THE NEXT YEAR, I PHOTOGRAPHED THEM ON SEVERAL DIFFERENT OCCASIONS IN LONDON AND ONCE IN LOS ANGELES.

EITHER I MUST HAVE MADE A BIG ENOUGH IMPRESSION ON THEM OR MY PHOTOGRAPHS DID; FOR BY THE TIME THEY RETURNED IN AUGUST 1988 FOR THE DONINGTON MONSTERS OF ROCK FESTIVAL, I REMEMBER DOUG GOLDSTEIN, THEIR TOUR MANAGER AT THE TIME, TELLING ME THAT AXL, WHO HAD DEVELOPED AN INTENSE DISLIKE FOR PHOTOGRAPHERS BY THEN, HAD DECIDED THAT THERE WERE ONLY TWO PHOTOGRAPHERS HE WANTED TO TAKE HIS PICTURES, AND I WAS ONE OF THEM.

OVER THE NEXT COUPLE OF YEARS THE BAND WENT TO HELL AND BACK. THEY WITHDREW FROM THE PUBLIC EYE AND IT WASN'T UNTIL JANUARY 1991 THAT THEY RE-EMERGED AFTER PARTING COMPANY WITH STEVEN ADLER, THEIR ORIGINAL DRUMMER. THEY WERE SCHEDULED TO PLAY THE ROCK IN RIO FESTIVAL IN RIO DE JANEIRO, BRAZIL, AT THE MARACANA STADIUM. DOUG GOLDSTEIN FAXED ME TO SAY THAT AXL WANTED ME TO GO TO RIO, AND SO IT WAS THAT MY LIFE BECAME ENTANGLED WITH THEIRS FOR THE NEXT EIGHT MONTHS — RIGHT UP TO WHEN IZZY STRADLIN LEFT THE BAND.

THE FOLLOWING PAGES OF PHOTOGRAPHS, MANY OF THEM UNPUBLISHED BEFORE, DOCUMENT SOME OF THEIR EARLY SHOWS AS WELL AS THE LATER ONES ON THE "GET IN THE RING MOTHERFUCKER" TOUR. I HOPE THEY CONVEY AN IMPRESSION OF WHAT IT WAS LIKE TO BE CLOSE TO THE BAND.

GEORGE CHIN, 1994.

I CAN'T QUITE REMEMBER IF I PHOTOGRAPHED GN'R AT THEIR FIRST MARQUEE SHOW, THE SECOND OR THE LAST. WHAT I DO REMEMBER WAS THAT IT WAS A SUMMER EVENING, IT WAS PACKED AND VERY HOT AND SWEATY.

SHOOTING AT THE OLD MARQUEE WAS ALWAYS VERY DIFFICULT BECAUSE THE STAGE WAS KNEE-HIGH AND IT WAS IMPOSSIBLE TO SEE MORE THAN THE HEADS OF THE BAND ABOVE THE HEADS OF THE AUDIENCE.

I WAS COMMISSIONED BY BURRN! — THE BIGGEST SELLING JAPANESE ROCK MAGAZINE — TO DO A COVER SHOOT WITH AXL FOR THEIR JANUARY 1988 ISSUE. GN'R WAS THEIR MOST PROMISING ACT IN 1988 TO MAKE IT BIG.

HE WAS WEARING A BERET ANGLED TO ONE SIDE AND HE REMINDED ME OF AN IRA TYPE WITHOUT THE DARK GLASSES... DEFINITELY AN ANGRY YOUNG MAN.

IT WAS OBVIOUS THAT FOR WHATEVER REASON, AXL JUST DID NOT WANT TO DO ANY PHOTOS THAT EVENING. HE WAS UNCO-OPERATIVE AND UNRESPONSIVE AND JUST GLARED AT THE CAMERA. I KNEW THE PHOTOS WERE NOT GOING TO BE GOOD SO I DIDN'T MAKE A MEAL OF IT AND GAVE UP AFTER ONE ROLL. WHEN I SHOWED HIM THE RESULTS, HE TOOK ONE LOOK AT THEM AND AGREED TO RE-SHOOT THE SESSION.

HE REAPPEARED TOTALLY PSYCHED UP WITH A REVAMPED LOOK — HIS FRINGE WAS NOW UNDER HIS TRADEMARK BANDANNA. HE WORE A LEATHER COAT AT FIRST AND AFTER HE WARMED UP, I ASKED HIM TO REMOVE HIS COAT AND FOLD HIS ARMS TO EMPHASISE HIS UNIQUE TATTOOS.

I KNEW THAT THIS WAS THE SHOT FOR THE COVER AND IT BECAME A TRADEMARK POSE FOR A WHILE.

"WE'RE A BAD-BOY BAND. WE'RE NOT AFRAID TO GO TO EXCESS WITH SUBSTANCES, SEXUALLY AND EVERYTHING ELSE. WE KNOW WE'RE ALWAYS GOING TO BE AT ODDS WITH PEOPLE ON SOMETHING. A LOT OF PEOPLE ARE AFRAID TO BE THAT WAY. WE'RE NOT. AND THE REASON IS THAT THE BANDS WHO HAVE MADE IT REAL BIG ARE THE BANDS WHO HAVE BEEN THAT WAY. AND GUNS N' ROSES PLAN ON MAKING IT REAL BIG."

AXL, JUNE 1987

## NOTTINGHAM ROCK CITY - AUTUMN '87

THAT NIGHT AT THE SHOW, IT WAS THE FIRST TIME THAT I EVER SAW
A SINGER SING HIS ANGER OUT ON STAGE. NO CUES, JUST RAW
VOCAL POWER AND A PERFORMANCE IN WHICH AXL STRUTTED AND
STOMPED AND SWIVELLED IN HIS CHARACTERISTIC WAY UNTIL
WHATEVER IT WAS THAT WAS BUGGING HIM WAS OUT OF HIS
SYSTEM AND THE ANGER SPENT .

19A 19B 20
FUJI-RHP

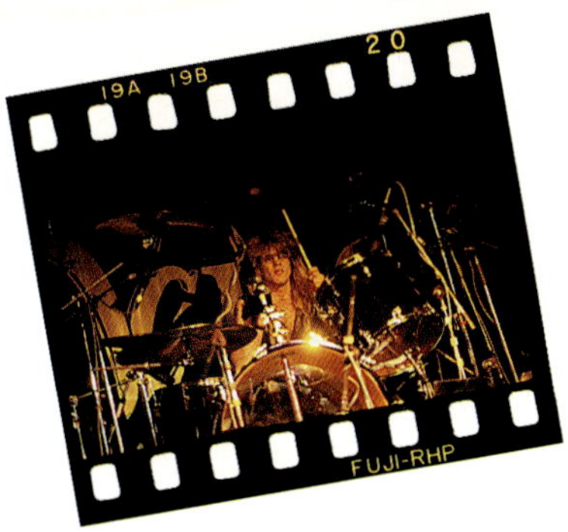

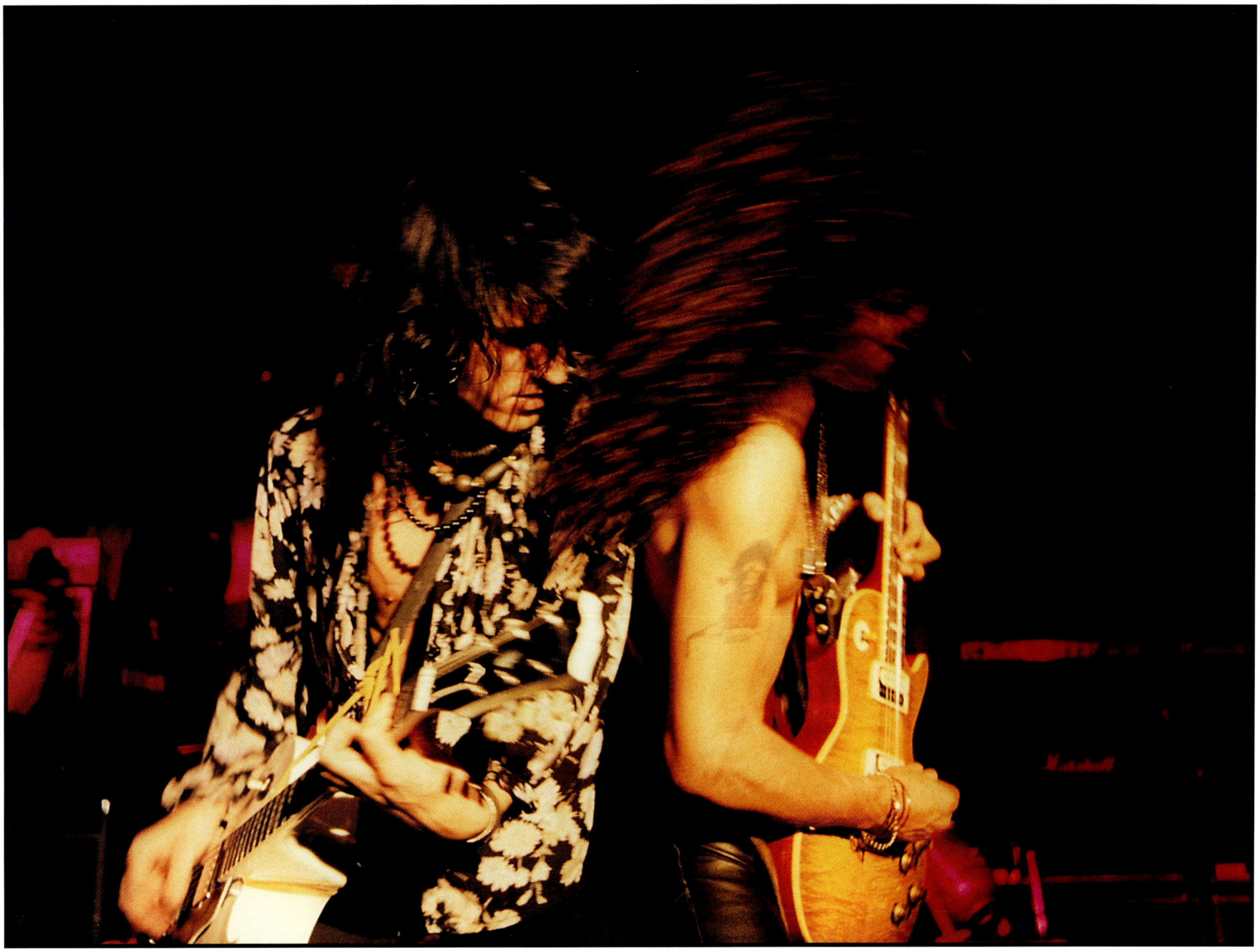

25
25A 25B

4B
FUJI
5
5A

RHP•216
5B
6
6A

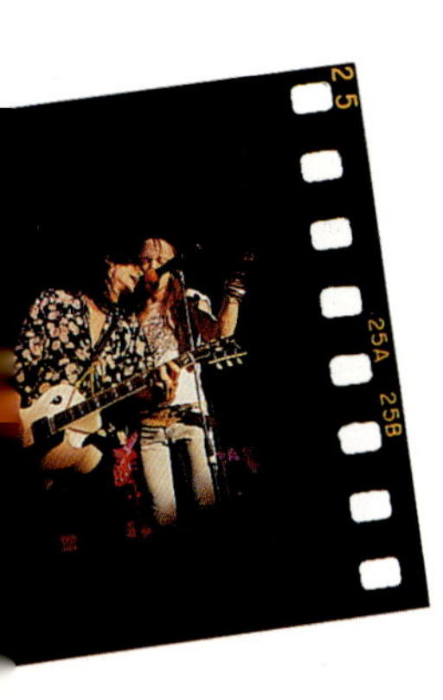

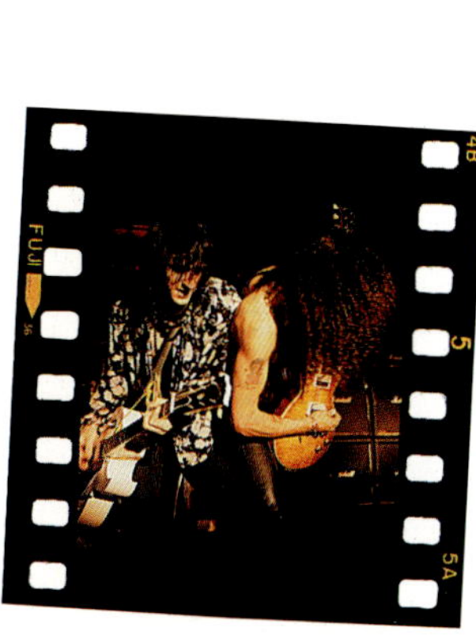

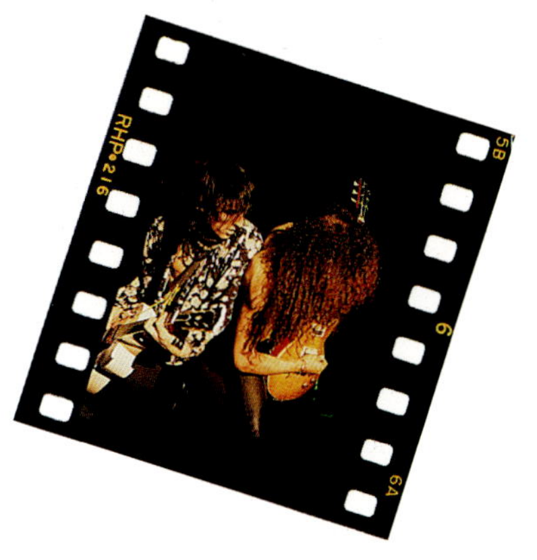

## HAMMERSMITH ODEON - OCTOBER '87

**THE SHORT FIVE DATE TOUR ENDED AT THE HAMMERSMITH ODEON AND THIS WAS THEIR MOST ACCOMPLISHED PERFORMANCE TO DATE. THE ROCK PRESS WERE SEDUCED.**

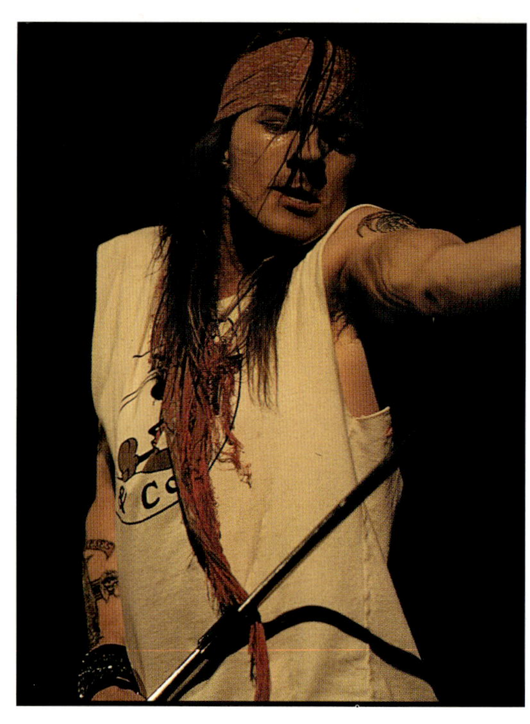

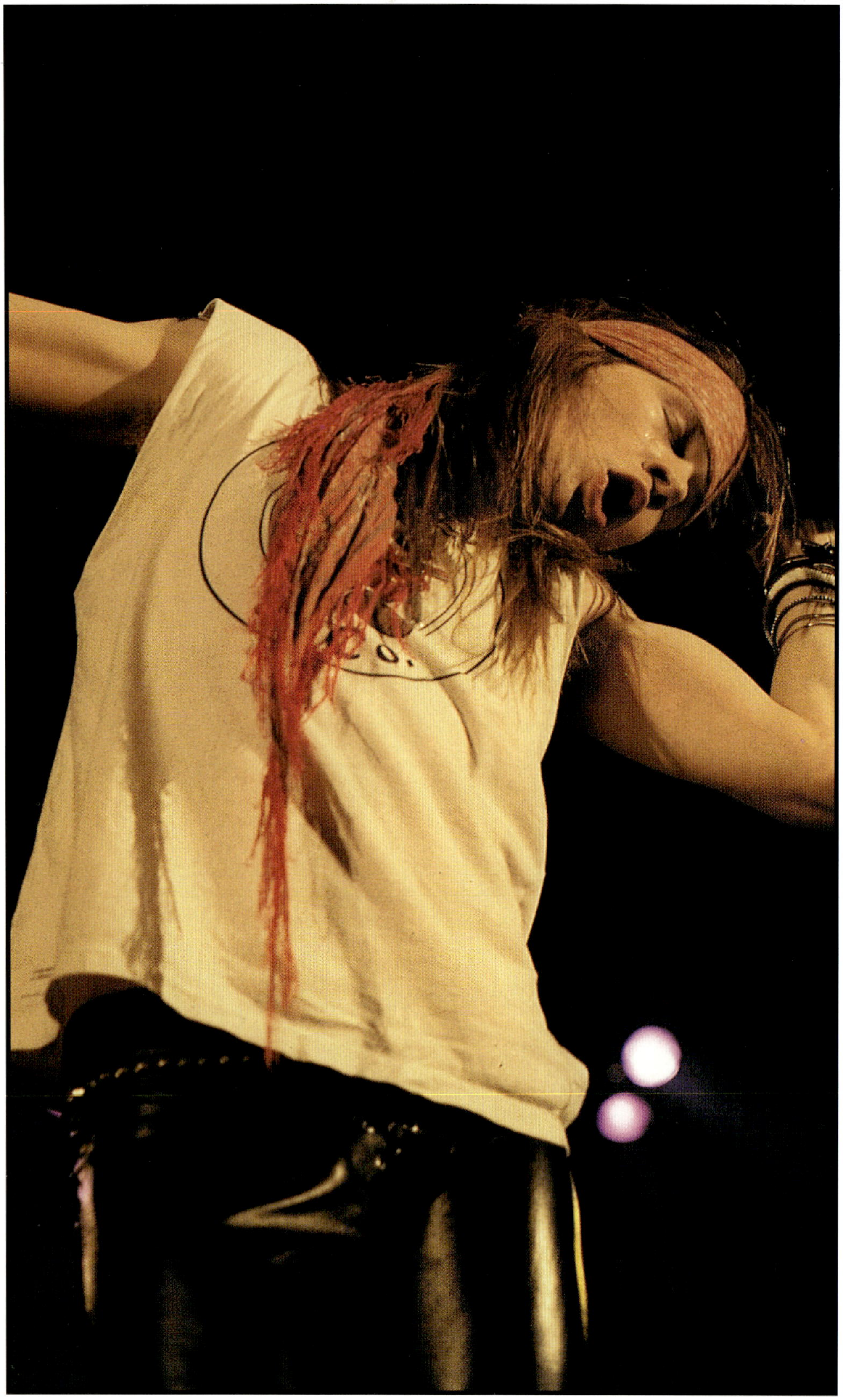

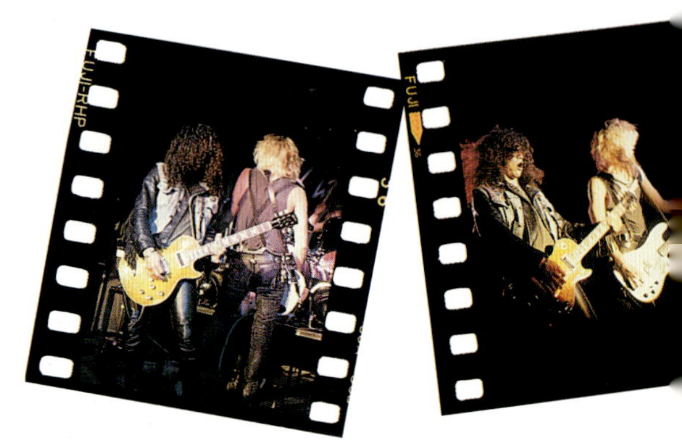

## IZZY

IZZY AND AXL WERE REALLY GOOD MATES — VERY LOYAL TO EACH OTHER. AXL RESPECTED IZZY'S OPINION AND MUSICAL IDEAS. IZZY WOULD NEVER, EVER, SLAG AXL OFF EVEN IF HE WAS PISSED OFF AT HIM. IZZY IS THE EPITOME OF A REAL COOL DUDE. HE IS HIS IMAGE — LIKE KEITH RICHARDS, HIS IDOL.

"I'VE BEEN STRAIGHT FOR A YEAR AND A HALF NOW. NO BOOZE, NO WEED, NOTHING. I JUST STOPPED COLD. I SAID, 'FUCK, I SHOULD GIVE THIS A SHOT'. WHEN I FINALLY STOPPED AND THEN STARTED GOING OUT, JUST RIDING AROUND ON A FUCKING BICYCLE, I THOUGHT 'WOW, THIS IS REALLY COOL. HOW DID I FORGET ALL THIS SIMPLE SHIT?' "

**IZZY, OCTOBER 1991**

THE BAND FLEW INTO ENGLAND ON CONCORD, RIGHT IN THE MIDDLE OF A TOUR OF THE USA SUPPORTING AEROSMITH. THEY ARRIVED FRIDAY EVENING AND WERE DUE TO FLY BACK FIRST THING SUNDAY MORNING.

IN BOTH EMOTIONAL AND COMMERCIAL TERMS, THEY WERE THE ONLY BAND WORTH SHOOTING AT DONINGTON THAT YEAR.

I DIDN'T SEE THEM BEFORE THEY WENT ON STAGE, BUT WHEN THEY DID APPEAR THE FIRST THING I NOTICED WAS THAT THEY NO LONGER LOOKED LIKE JUST ANY OTHER LA BAND. THEIR PERFORMANCE WAS FASTER, MORE FRENETIC NOW AND THEIR WHOLE IMAGE SEEMED TO HAVE MOVED AWAY FROM THE LA GLAM THING. THE EXPRESSION 'SLEAZE' WAS COINED TO DESCRIBE THIS NEW IMAGE.

BACKSTAGE, WHEN I SAW AXL HE LOOKED A LOT THINNER.

AFTER THE SHOW, DOUG GOLDSTEIN ASKED ME NOT TO TELL THE BAND THAT TWO FANS HAD BEEN TRAMPLED TO DEATH DURING THEIR SET. THEY FLEW BACK TO AMERICA ON CONCORD NOT KNOWING OF THE TERRIBLE TRAGEDY THAT HAD OCCURRED.

DONINGTON '88

EVERY BAND GETS BOTTLED AT DONINGTON, AND GN'R WERE NO EXCEPTION. THIS WAS THE FIRST TIME THEY HAD PLAYED AT AN ENGLISH OUTDOOR FESTIVAL AND THEY WEREN'T FAMILIAR WITH THE CUSTOM OF BOTTLING PISS AND HURLING IT ON STAGE. SLASH TOLD ME HE PICKED UP A BOTTLE WHICH LOOKED LIKE IT HAD BEER IN IT. HE PUT IT TO HIS MOUTH AND TOOK A SWIG. WHAT WENT INTO HIS MOUTH WAS NOT BEER. WELCOME TO DONINGTON!

AS USUAL, LEMMY WAS LIGGING.

JOHN JACKSON AND ALAN NIVEN, GN'R'S AGENT AND MANAGER AT THE TIME.

AXL AND SLASH WITH LARS ULRICH AND DAVE MUSTAINE.

KODAK EPD 2036
KODAK EPD 5036

THE LAST TIME I SHOT STEVE WAS WHEN HE TURNED UP WITH SLASH
AND DUFF FOR A MAGAZINE AWARD IN L.A. IN APRIL '89.

STEVE HAD JUST HAD THIS KICK DRUM SKIN SPECIALLY MADE, BUT HE NEVER HAD A CHANCE TO USE IT.

## STEVEN ADLER

STEVEN, LIKE ALL DRUMMERS, WAS A LITTLE BIT EXTROVERT AND LOVED BEING FAMOUS AND RECOGNISED.

THE BAND NEVER TALKED ABOUT STEVEN'S SACKING AT ALL APART FROM WHAT THEY SAID IN THE PRESS RELEASE AND OFFICIAL STORIES. EITHER THEIR LAWYERS TOLD THEM NOT TO SPEAK OR THE EXPERIENCE WAS TRAUMATIC.

GN'R WERE NO LONGER THE "MOST DANGEROUS BAND IN THE WORLD" BUT 'GUNS N'FUCKIN' ROSES INC – G'N'F'R'.

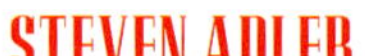

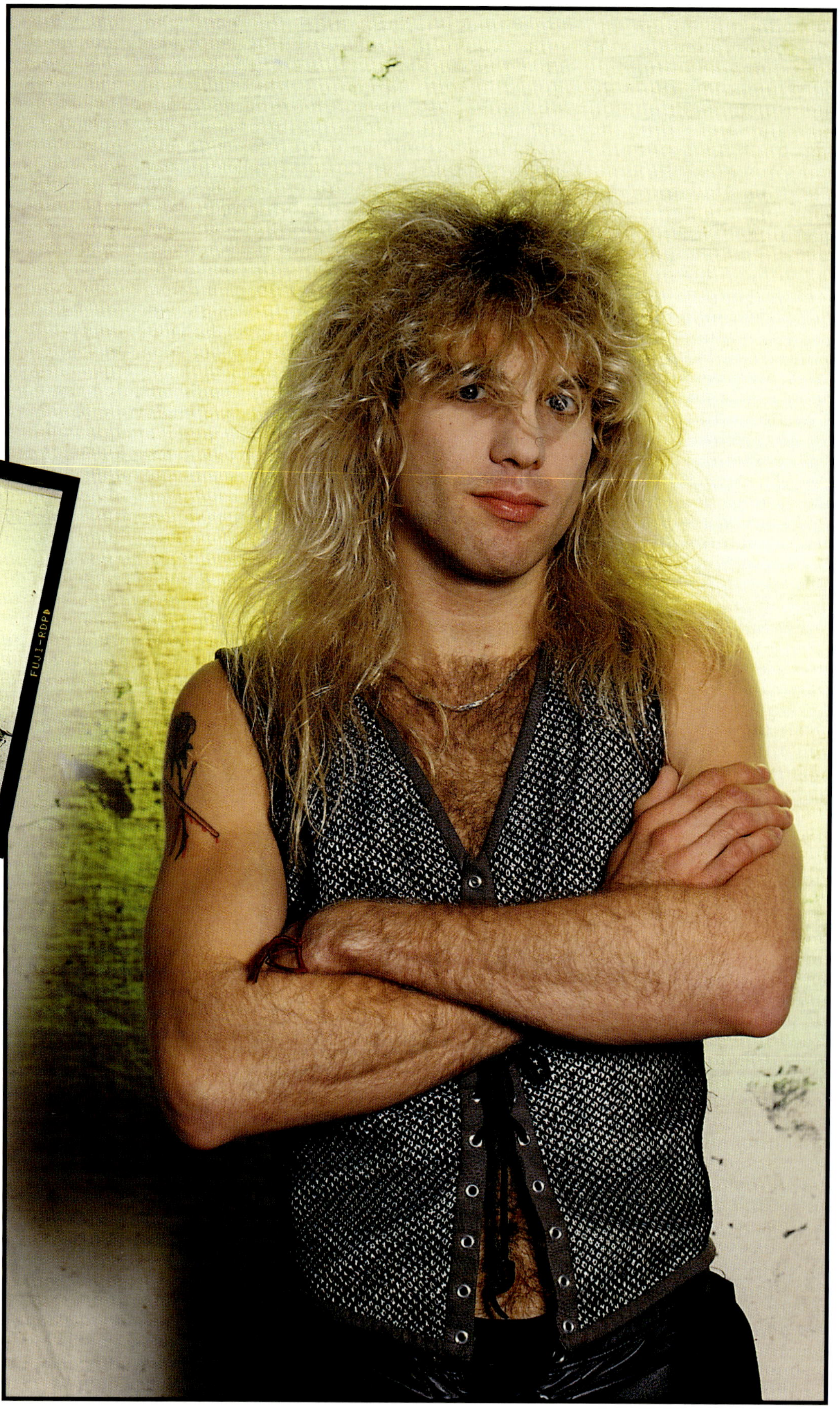

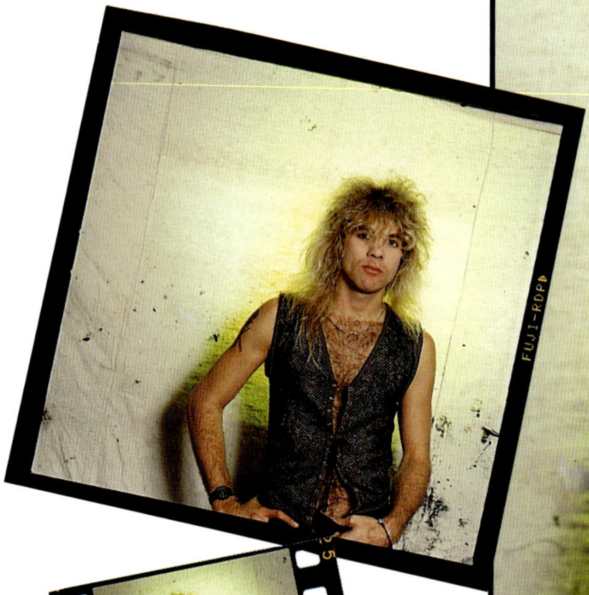


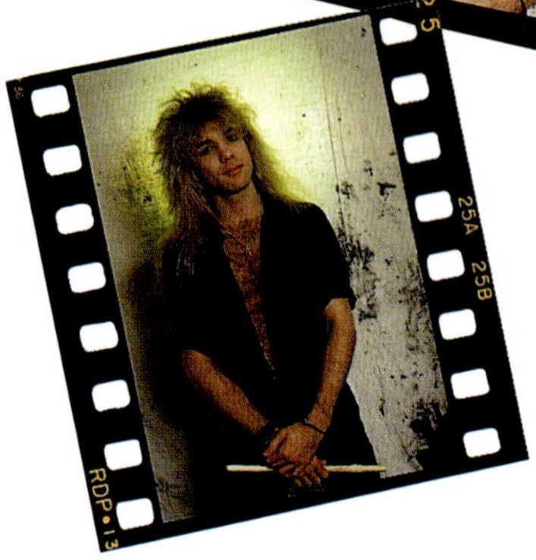

"AS AMAZING AS IT SEEMS IN THIS DRUG-FREE, EXERCISE AND HEALTH AGE, THERE'S A BUNCH OF US WHO ARE STILL CLINGING FAST TO THE LATE '60S AND '70S. BUT STEVE NEVER GREW UP TO THE FACT THAT IT'S NOT ALL JUST SEX, DRUGS AND ROCK'N'ROLL. TO HIM IT WAS A BIG FANTASY AND WE TOOK CARE OF HIM. AND NOW HE'S ON HIS OWN."

**SLASH, FEBRUARY 1991**

Rock in Rio II
CREDENCIAL DE ACESSO
N° 000876
20
ARTIST

18/01
SEXTA
FRIDAY
19/01
SABADO
SATURDAY
20/01
DOMINGO
SUNDAY
22/01
TERÇA
TUESDAY
23/01
QUARTA
WEDNESDAY
PRINCE
INXS
GUNS N'ROSES
JOE COCKER
BILLY IDOL
ROBERT PLANT
NEW KIDS ON
THE BLOCK
GUNS N'ROSES
COLIN HAY
SANTANA
FAITH NO MORE
RUN DMC
JUDAS PRIEST

THIS WAS THE FIRST TIME I HAD MET UP WITH THEM SINCE 1989 AND BY NOW STEVEN ADLER HAD BEEN REPLACED BY MATT SORUM.

MATT TOLD ME THAT AXL HAD NEVER SANG IN FRONT OF HIM DURING REHEARSALS FOR RIO, SO THE GIG REALLY WAS THE FIRST TIME HE'D EVER PLAYED WITH GUNS N' ROSES.

OF ALL THE BANDS THAT PLAYED ROCK IN RIO 1991, GUNS N'ROSES WAS THE ONLY ONE THAT SOLD OUT ON BOTH NIGHTS.

## ROCK IN RIO II
## GUNS N' ROSES ROOMING LIST

Goldstein, Doug (Tour Manager)    1201/1203
Skelerseth, Dale (Opie)    1113
Reese, John    1205
*A* Omnibone, Bob    1101
*S* Likesheet, Luke    1115
*D* Likesheet, Phil    1118
*I* Chama, Dali    1114
*M* Wassaint, Ian    1100
Reed, Daren    1133
Campbell, Curtis    1126
Day, Adam    1111
Dowle, Timmy    1128

1109
1108
1110
1132
1127
1206
1129
1131
1107
1124
1130

1105
1112
Green, Willie    1122
Zucker, John    1106
Stalnaker, Ron    1119

1830 SO. ROBERTSON BLVD., SUITE 201, LOS ANGELES, CA 90035 (213) 204-5890

RIO WAS WILD. EVERYWHERE THE BAND WENT, BODYGUARDS HAD TO
GO WITH THEM. THEY COULDN'T GO ANYWHERE WITHOUT GETTING
MOBBED. IT GOT TO THE STAGE WHERE SLASH DECIDED TO WEAR A
SKULL MASK AS A GIMMICK TO SEE IF HE WOULD BE RECOGNISED.

# MATT MEETS JESUS

MATT WENT FOR A DAY OUT UP THE CORCOVADO MOUNTAIN TO SAY HELLO TO THE STATUE OF JESUS. HE WAS MOBBED BY FANS SHOUTING GUNS N'ROSES. HOW THE HELL DID THEY KNOW HE WAS THE NEW DRUMMER? THERE WERE NO PRESS SHOTS AVAILABLE. IT WAS UNCANNY.

213·650·6530

# SKATEBOARDING WITH IZZY

IZZY WAS GETTING INTO SKATEBOARDING. HE WOULD GET UP AROUND 8AM IN THE MORNING TO AVOID THE CROWDS AND HEAD FOR THE NEAREST RINK.

MOST OF THE TIME SLASH HUNG OUT BY THE POOL. ON ONE OF THE DAY'S OFF HE WENT TO VISIT A SERPENTARIUM IN SAO PAULO. EVERYWHERE SLASH WENT HIS PERSONAL BODYGUARD, RON STALNAKER, WENT WITH HIM. RON LOOKED LIKE A PUMPED UP VERSION OF SLASH — AND EVERYONE NICKNAMED HIM 'SLASH ON STEROIDS'.

SLASH PREFERRED JOHN JACKSON'S HAT WHICH HAD A BULLET HOLE IN THE SIDE.

KEEPING COOL WITH SLASH

DUFF'S GIRLFRIEND CAME OUT TO RIO WITH HIM, SO HE HUNG OUT
MOST OF THE TIME IN HIS ROOM GETTING LAID. I HAD TO GATECRASH
THEIR LITTLE SCENE TO HASSLE HIM TO DO SOME PICS. WE ENDED UP
DOING THEM ON THE BALCONY AND WHEN MATT POPPED IN, I
SUGGESTED WE TAKE OVER THE BED. ONLY THING, HIS GIRLFRIEND
DIDN'T WANT TO JOIN IN.

DIZZY SAID HIS WILDEST DREAMS HAD COME TRUE. HE HAD NEVER TOURED BEFORE, AND HE WAS THE LUCKIEST PERSON IN THE WORLD TO HAVE HAD THE CHANCE TO JOIN GUNS N'ROSES. HE WAS ECSTATIC. HE HAD JUST SPLIT UP WITH HIS WIFE AND HE ALWAYS HAD A DIFFERENT GIRL WHENEVER I SAW HIM.

EuVOU

# G N' R SOUNDCHECK

SOUNDCHECK IN RIO WAS THE FIRST TIME THAT THE NEW LINE-UP HAD EVER REHEARSED WITH AXL. AFTER A COUPLE OF NUMBERS WITH MATT ON DRUMS AND DIZZY ON KEYBOARDS, ALL THE DOUBTS VANISHED, AND EVERYONE KNEW IT WAS GOING TO BE GOOD. YOU COULD SEE THE SMILES.

BRAZILIAN TV-GLOBO WAS SECRETLY FILMING THE SOUNDCHECK WITHOUT PERMISSION. TOUR MANAGER DOUG GOLDSTEIN SUSSED WHAT WAS GOING ON, AND WRESTLED THE VIDEO TAPE OFF ONE OF THE CAMERA OPS. HE WAS IMMEDIATELY SURROUNDED BY ABOUT THIRTY HEAVY LOOKING BRAZILIAN MAFIA TYPES. DOUG THREW THE TAPE TO JOHN REESE, WHO WAS HEAD OF SECURITY AT THE TIME AND SHOUTED TO HIM TO GET THE HELL OUT OF THERE WITH IT. THE CREW SAW WHAT WAS GOING ON AND CAME OVER TO BACK DOUG UP. FOR ONE MOMENT IT LOOKED VERY DANGEROUS, BEFORE ONE OF THE INTERPRETERS CALMED THINGS DOWN.

AXL LOOKED REALLY HEALTHY AND TANNED AND HAD OBVIOUSLY BEEN WORKING OUT. HE TOLD ME HE'D BEEN DOING TWO HUNDRED SIT-UPS A DAY, AND IT SHOWED. COMPARED TO DONINGTON, HE LOOKED REALLY GREAT!

AXL CAME ON WEARING A WHITE GUNS N'ROSES JACKET HE'D HAD MADE. AFTER A COUPLE OF SONGS HE TOOK IT OFF AND BY THE END OF THE SHOW IT HAD DISAPPEARED, NEVER TO BE SEEN AGAIN. SOMEONE HAD TAKEN IT AS A SOUVENIR.

THE SECOND RIO GIG WAS THE BEST EVER GUNS N'ROSES GIG I EVER SAW. EVERYONE WAS ON A HIGH AFTERWARDS. AXL COULDN'T SLEEP THAT NIGHT AND THREW A PARTY IN HIS ROOM ON THE SPUR OF THE MOMENT. EVERYONE WITH THE BAND WAS WOKEN UP TO COME TO THE PARTY, EVEN BILLY IDOL WHO WAS STAYING IN THE SAME HOTEL.

CBGB
&
OMFUG
Home of Underground Rock
FUJI RHP
29

FUJI RHP

# GET IN THE RING TOUR

I FLEW IN TO MILWAUKEE FOR THE FIRST DATE ON MAY 25, 1991, AND THEY SENT A STRETCH LIMO TO MEET ME AT THE AIRPORT TO TAKE ME TO ALPINE VALLEY, THE FIRST GIG, WHICH WAS AN HOUR'S DRIVE AWAY.

GUNS N' ROSES' HOTEL WAS SET ON A LAKESIDE, WITH PRIVATE CHALETS IN LANDSCAPED GROUNDS. THE BAND HAD TAKEN OVER A WHOLE SECTION.

THE PLANE WAS A BOEING 737, CHARTERED FROM MGM.  IT HAD A
LOUNGE AREA AT THE FRONT AND A BAR IN THE CENTRE.  AT THE REAR
WERE COMPARTMENTS WITH SEATS LIKE IN A FIRST CLASS RAILWAY
CARRIAGE. WHENEVER THE STEWARDESSES ASKED EVERYONE TO
TAKE A SEAT FOR TAKE-OFF AND TO FASTEN SAFETY BELTS, AXL
WOULD IMMEDIATELY GET UP AND WALK UP AND DOWN THE AISLE.

EACH OF THE BAND HAD THEIR OWN BODYGUARD BUT DUFF HATED
HAVING A SHADOW WHEREVER HE WENT. SOMETIMES, IN THE MIDDLE
OF THE NIGHT, HE WOULD LEAVE THE HOTEL AND GO CHECK OUT SOME
ROCK CLUBS IN WHATEVER TOWN THE BAND WERE STAYING IN. THE
POOR GUY'S JOB WAS ON THE LINE AND YOU WOULD OFTEN SEE HIM
WANDERING ROUND THE LOBBY ASKING IF ANYONE HAD SEEN DUFF.
WHEN HE REALISED THAT DUFF WAS NOWHERE IN THE HOTEL, HE HAD
TO GO LOOK FOR HIM IN ALL THOSE PLACES HE KNEW DUFF WOULD BE
HANGING OUT IN. HE ALWAYS FOUND HIM!

THE **GM** GOLD MOUNTAIN *Intercharter* GROUP, INC.

FAX

## Guns 'N Roses

| Date | Route | Depart | Arrive |
|---|---|---|---|
| Jun 12 | Harrisburg(MDT) -Philadelphia | 1700 | 1800 |
| Jun 14 | Philadelphia-New York City | 1700 | 1815 |
| Jun 18 | New York (JFK) - Washington DC (DCA) | 1700 | 1800 |
| Jun 22 | Washington DC (DCA)-Hampton | 1700 | 1800 |
| Jun 23 | Hampton-Charlotte,NC | 1700 | 1800 |
| Jun 25 | Charlotte, NC (CLT)-Greensboro,NC (GSO) | 1700 | 1800 |
| Jun 26 | Greensboro,NC (GSO)-Knoxville, TN | 1700 | |
| Jun 28 | Knoxville, TN -Lexington,KY(LEX) | 1700 | |
| Jun 30 | Lexington,KY(LEX)-Birmingham,Al (BHM) | 1700 | |
| Jul 1 | Birmingham,AL (BHM)-St Louis, MO (STL) | 1700 | |
| Jul 3 | St Louis, MO (STL)-Chicago, IL | 1700 | |
| Jul 6 | Chicago, IL- Kansas City,MO (MCI) | 1700 | |
| Jul 7 | Kansas City,MO (MCI)-Dallas,TX (Love field) | 1700 | 1835 |
| Jul 11 | Dallas, TX (Love field) - Denver, CO (DEN) | 1700 | 1800 |
| Jul 14 | Denver, CO (DEN) - Seattle, WA (BFI) | 1700 | 1848 |
| Jul 18 | Seattle, WA (BFI) - San Francisco(SFO) | 1700 | 1900 |
| Jul 22 | San Francisco(SFO) - Sacramento (SMF) | 1700 | 1845 |

AT ABOUT THE SAME TIME THAT THE DOORS FILM BY OLIVER STONE WAS RELEASED IN THE USA IN 1991, THERE WERE SEVERAL BOOKS OUT AND AXL HAD READ ALL OF THEM AND SEEN THE FILM. HE IDENTIFIED WITH JIM MORRISON TO THE EXTENT THAT DURING THE MIDDLE OF THE 1991 EUROPEAN LEG OF THE TOUR, HE MADE HIS OWN PERSONAL PILGRIMAGE TO PARIS TO VISIT MORRISON'S GRAVE.

CAMPAIGN AGAINST MARIJUANA
PROHIBITION

DOUG GOLDSTEIN INSISTED THAT THE FORD T-SHIRT DISAPPEAR
FROM SLASH'S WARDROBE IN CASE THE MOTOR COMPANY JOINED
IN THE WAR OF THE ROSES ON THE OPPOSITE SIDE.

WITHIN ONE WEEK OF THE TOUR STARTING IN AMERICA, ALL THESE PEOPLE CAME OUT OF THE WOODWORK AND WENT ON CNN AND ABC ACCUSING AXL OF KICKING THEIR DOG OR CREATING A DISTURBANCE OR MAKING A NOISE NEXT DOOR... ANYTHING TO GET THEIR 15 MINUTES OF FAME OR A QUICK SETTLEMENT AT AXL'S EXPENSE.

"IN THE WHOLE SCHEME OF THINGS WE'RE JUST A ROCK'N'ROLL BAND. WE'RE SITTING HERE SMOKING CIGS AND HAVING A DRINK, THEN WE GO HOME, FUCK OUR GIRLFRIENDS AND GO TO BED. THEN WE WAKE UP, GO BACK TO THE STUDIO TO DO ANOTHER SONG OR TWO. FUCK MAN, WE'VE BEEN ASKED TO COMMENT ON THINGS TOTALLY OUT OF OUR LEAGUE AND WE'RE APPARENTLY SUPPOSED TO KNOW EVERYTHING ABOUT EVERYTHING, JUST BECAUSE WE'VE SOLD A FEW ALBUMS. FUCK, WHAT DO I KNOW ABOUT NELSON MANDELA BEING FREE."

**DUFF, APRIL 1990**

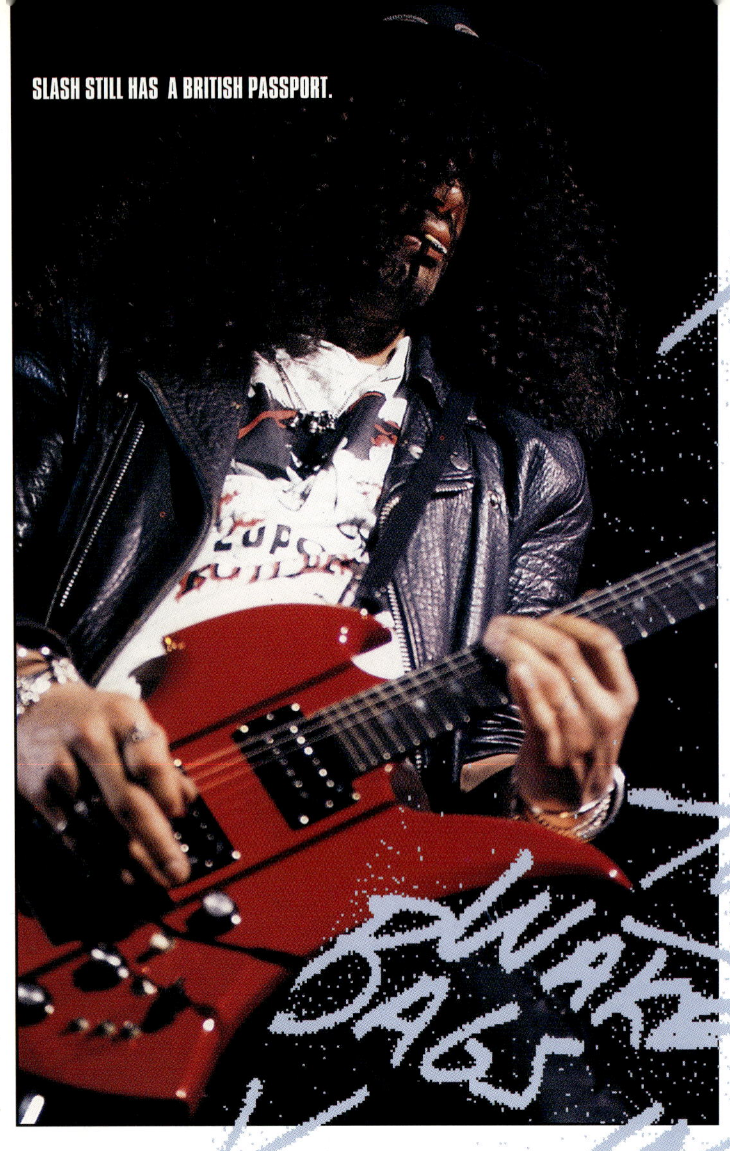

SLASH STILL HAS A BRITISH PASSPORT.

INDIANAPOLIS IS WHERE AXL AND IZZY GREW UP. AT THIS GIG, AXL SENT A STRETCH TO COLLECT HIS GRANNY AND FAMILY FROM LAFAYETTE, TO COME TO THE GIG. THE DRIVER HAD ORDERS TO BRING BACK ICE-CREAM AND PIZZAS FROM THIS ONE STORE IN LAFAYETTE WHERE AXL USED TO HANG OUT WHEN HE WAS A KID, AND AFTER THE SHOW, AXL AND HIS FAMILY HAD A REAL HOMELY REUNION. AXL'S GRANNY WAS AN OLDER FEMALE VERSION OF HIM. SHE KNEW ALL THE WORDS TO ALL THE GUNS N' ROSES SONGS AND SHE SANG ALONG AT THE GIG.

IN INDIANAPOLIS, THE BAND STAYED IN THE SAME HOTEL WHERE MIKE TYSON WAS ACCUSED OF RAPING DESIREE WASHINGTON. AXL WAS IN THE SAME SUITE.

I ONLY EVER HEARD AXL TRASHING A ROOM ONCE. HE WAS REALLY MAD ABOUT SOMETHING AND HE TOOK IT OUT ON THE SUITE. DOUG GOLDSTEIN HAD TO SMOOTH IT OUT WITH THE HOTEL MANAGER AFTERWARDS.

GET IN THE SHOWER
MOTHERFUCKER!
DAILY INFO SHEET
TUESDAY MAY 28
WAKE UP 10 00 AM
BAGS IN HALL 10 30 AM
VANS TO AIRPORT 12 NOON
FLIGHT TO INDY 1 00

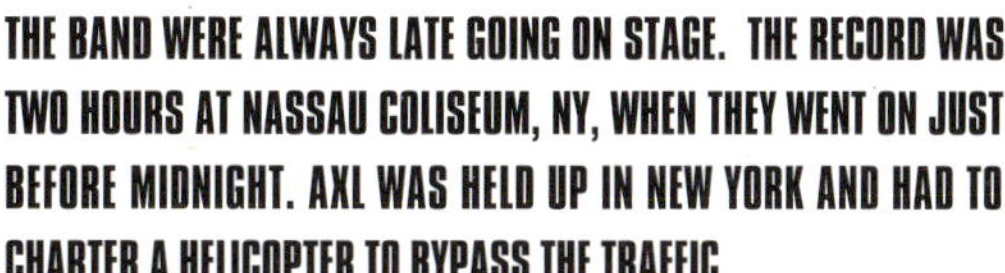

THE BAND WERE ALWAYS LATE GOING ON STAGE. THE RECORD WAS
TWO HOURS AT NASSAU COLISEUM, NY, WHEN THEY WENT ON JUST
BEFORE MIDNIGHT. AXL WAS HELD UP IN NEW YORK AND HAD TO
CHARTER A HELICOPTER TO BYPASS THE TRAFFIC.

MATT ALWAYS HAD AT LEAST TWO GIRLS GOING BACK TO HIS HOTEL
ROOM AFTER THE SHOW FOR A PRIVATE PARTY.  ONCE I COUNTED
TEN.

AT EVERY AIRPORT, WE WERE MET BY THREE STRETCH LIMOS, ONE FOR AXL, ONE FOR SLASH AND DUFF AND THE OTHER FOR MATT AND DIZZY (IZZY TRAVELLED SEPARATELY). ALSO, THERE WERE TWO MINI-VANS FOR EVERYONE ELSE THAT TRAVELLED WITH THEM, AND A TRUCK FOR THE LUGGAGE. QUITE A CONVOY.

GET IN THE SHOW MOTHERFUCKER

DAILY INFO SHEET

WEDNESDAY MAY

WE ARE IN

SCHEDULE IS AS FOL

2:30 PM
3:30 PM
4:00 PM
7:15 PM
8:45 PM
11:00 PM

(317) 773-5

ON STAGE

CURFEW

PRODUCTION #'S

YOU GUYS WERE LAST NIGHT FUCKIN' AWESOME

KEEP ANYTHING

PICK UP YOUR

THE MONITORS WERE USED ON STAGE, NOT BECAUSE AXL COULDN'T REMEMBER THE WORDS, BUT BECAUSE EVERYONE DID SO MUCH RUNNING AND MOVING AROUND THAT THEY WERE A REFERENCE POINT AS TO WHERE THEY WERE WITH THE LYRICS. THE STAGE WAS HUGE, AND NOTHING WAS CHOREOGRAPHED. IT HAPPENED AS YOU SAW IT.

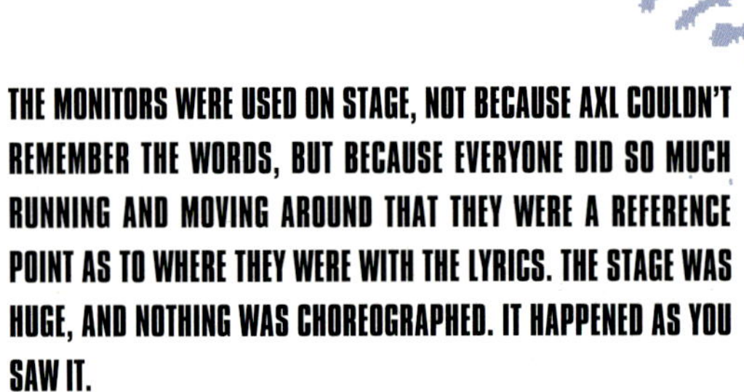

RON STALNAKER LOOKED LIKE SLASH ON STEROIDS. HERE HE IS WITH DUFF.

CURTIS CAMPBELL, AXL'S ROADIE WITH TOUR MANAGER JOHN REESE (RIGHT).

DOUG GOLDSTEIN SOMETIMES STOOD IN FOR AXL
AT SOUNDCHECKS.

ONCE IN DALLAS, WE ALL WENT TO A LOCAL ROCK CLUB AND WERE HANGING OUT IN A PRIVATE ROOM WITH SOME OF THE GUYS FROM PANTERA AND SKID ROW. THE LOCAL POLICE KNEW GUNS N'ROSES WERE IN TOWN AND WHEN THEY SAW THE LIMOS IN THE CAR PARK, THEY FIGURED THE BAND WERE INSIDE, SO THEY BUSTED THE PLACE, OBVIOUSLY TO GET ON PRIME TIME TV. BUT THE BODYGUARDS HAD SEEN THEIR BLUE LIGHTS FLASHING OUTSIDE THE CLUB AND GOT US OUT THROUGH A SIDE ENTRANCE WHILE THE COPS CAME THROUGH THE FRONT DOOR. FUNNY THING IS, NO-ONE WAS DOING ANYTHING ILLEGAL. LIKE MATT SAID, "NOTHING IS MADE UP. EVERYTHING THAT HAPPENS IS FOR REAL."

"THIS BAND IS WHAT IT IS. IT AIN'T NO BULLSHIT. IT ISN'T SITTING AROUND THINKING UP IDEAS FOR PUBLICITY. THIS STUFF REALLY HAPPENS! THEY'RE JUST BEING THEMSELVES. SO THIS IS IT, TAKE IT OR LEAVE IT, LOVE IT OR HATE IT, THAT'S WHY IT WORKS."

MATT, SEPTEMBER 1991

"EVERY NIGHT'S A FUCKING PARTY, MAN. CHICKS, BEER, YOU NAME IT. TAKE ANY CHICK YOU WANT, MAN. IT'S LIKE BEING IN A CANDY STORE."

MATT, OCTOBER 1991

AXL HAD JUMPED OFF A SPEAKER IN NEW YORK DURING A WARM-UP GIG AND DAMAGED HIS FOOT WHEN HE LANDED.

LATER THAT NIGHT, HE HAD HIS FOOT TAKEN CARE OF BY A PHYSIO FROM THE LOCAL FOOTBALL TEAM. IT WAS ENCASED IN A SPECIAL HARNESS WHICH ENABLED HIM TO WALK WITHOUT HIS FOOT ACTUALLY TOUCHING THE GROUND. HE WAS REALLY PLEASED WITH IT AND PRACTISED A FEW LEAPS IN THE HOTEL CORRIDOR.

FUJI RHP

THE WEMBLEY SHOW IN AUGUST 1991 WAS VERY HEAVY AND INTENSE. AT THE PREVIOUS SHOW IN MUNICH AXL HAD WALKED OFF STAGE – NOT FOR THE FIRST TIME – AFTER THE FIRST FEW SONGS AND DID NOT COME BACK ON FOR ALMOST HALF AN HOUR. THE PROMOTER HAD THE PRESENCE OF MIND TO GO ON STAGE AND ANNOUNCE THAT AXL HAD BEEN TAKEN ILL, WHILE DOUG PERSUADED HIM TO GO ON WITH THE SHOW. EVERYONE FELT THAT THIS WAS ANOTHER POTENTIAL RIOT SITUATION AND BY THE TIME THEY GOT TO WEMBLEY, IZZY WAS VERY UNHAPPY. EVERYONE FELT THAT THE BAND WERE GOING TO SPLIT BECAUSE IZZY HAD DECIDED HE WANTED OUT OF THE UNHOLY MESS. THEY WERE ACTUALLY WITHIN ONE MEETING OF IZZY LEAVING.

"WE WERE REBELS. WE ARE REBELS, AND THERE WEREN'T ANY REBELS AROUND IN THE EARLY '80s. FUCK, EVEN PUNK GOT TO BE A FASHION, AND THEN IT WAS DEAD. SO THE WHOLE ELEMENT OF ROCK, THAT WHOLE ATTITUDE DISAPPEARED. WE BROUGHT IT BACK IN A WAY. KIDS GOT INTO IT. ALL THE WAY FROM THE LITTLE KIDS WHO DON'T WANNA TAKE A BATH AT NIGHT TO TEENAGERS WHO ARE GENERALLY FUCKED UP ANYWAY, RIGHT THROUGH TO PEOPLE WHO RELATE TO THIS SHIT FROM THEIR YOUTH."

**SLASH, APRIL 1990**

AXL'S BODYGUARD, EARL, ONCE RISKED HIS LIFE TO PROTECT AXL FROM SOMEONE WITH A GUN.

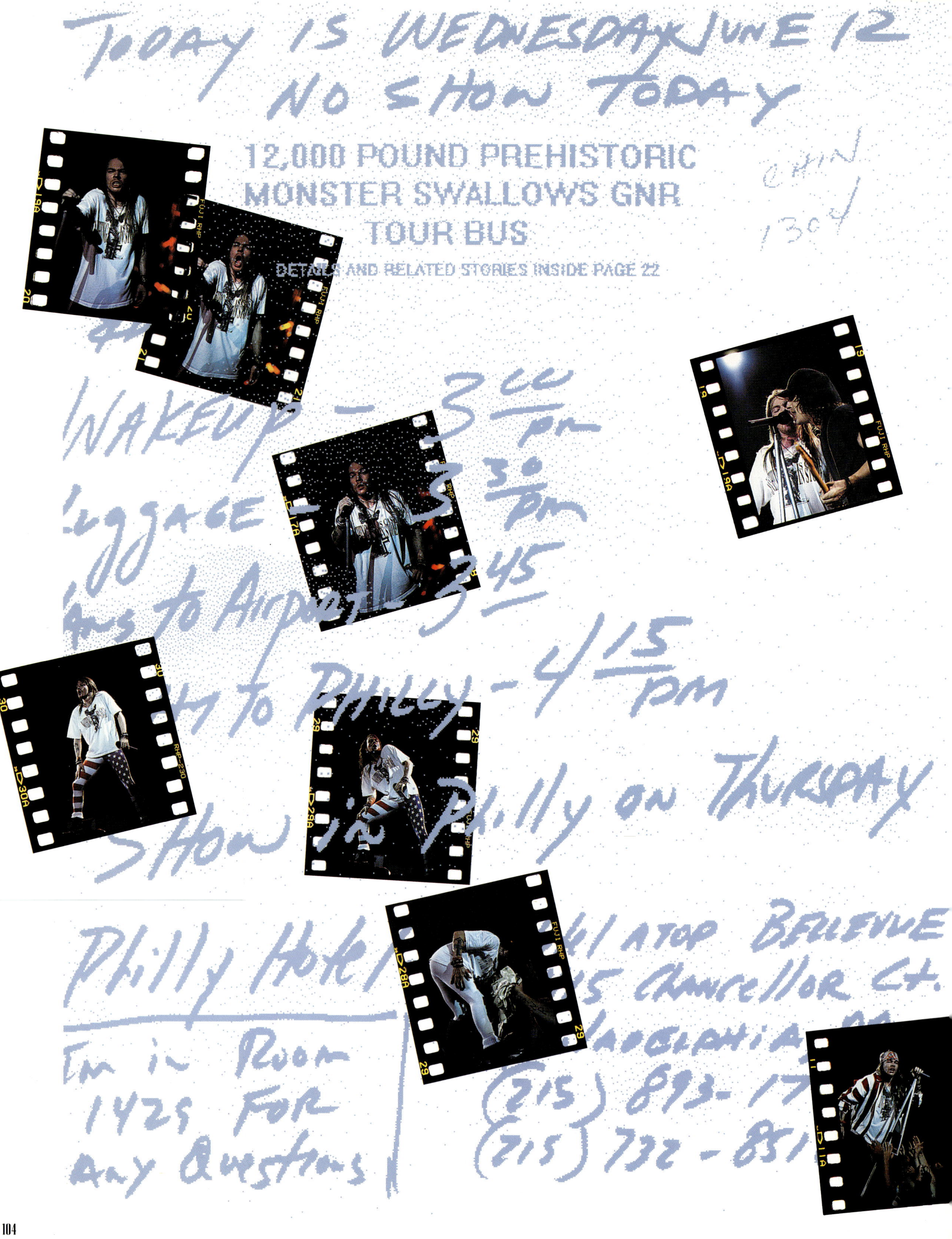

TODAY IS WEDNESDAY JUNE 12
NO SHOW TODAY

12,000 POUND PREHISTORIC
MONSTER SWALLOWS GNR
TOUR BUS

DETAILS AND RELATED STORIES INSIDE PAGE 22

CHIN
1304

WAKE UP - 3:00 PM
luggage - 3:30 PM
Bus to Airport - 3:45
Fly to Philly - 4:15 PM
Show in Philly on THURSDAY

Philly Hotel / atop BELLEVUE
5 Chancellor Ct.
Philadelphia PA
(215) 893-1...
(215) 732-851...

I'm in Room
1425 FOR
any Questions

THERE WAS ALWAYS AN AFTER SHOW PARTY TO WHICH CHOSEN GIRLS WERE INVITED. THERE WERE SO MANY GIRLS WANTING TO GET NEAR THE BAND THAT THEY WERE THROWING THEMSELVES AT ANYONE WHO COULD GET THEM BACKSTAGE. EVEN THE SUPPORT BAND'S CREW WERE PULLING.

DURING THE INTERVAL, SOME OF THE CREW GUYS WOULD GO OUT INTO THE AUDIENCE AND PICK THE GIRLS FOR THE AFTERSHOW PARTY. THEY WOULD TELL THEM TO COME TO THE BACKSTAGE DOOR AND WAIT. THEN JOHN REESE, WHO WAS BY THEN THE TOUR MANAGER, WOULD GO OUT AND MAKE THE FINAL SELECTION. THOSE LEFT OUTSIDE WOULD HANG AROUND FOR HOURS, TRYING TO LATCH ONTO ANYONE WHO COULD GET THEM INSIDE. YOU COULD JUST TAKE YOUR PICK.

'NOVEMBER RAIN' WAS AXL'S SONG. HE LOVED PLAYING THE PIANO AND SINGING THIS LIVE.

RHP-230
6
6
6A

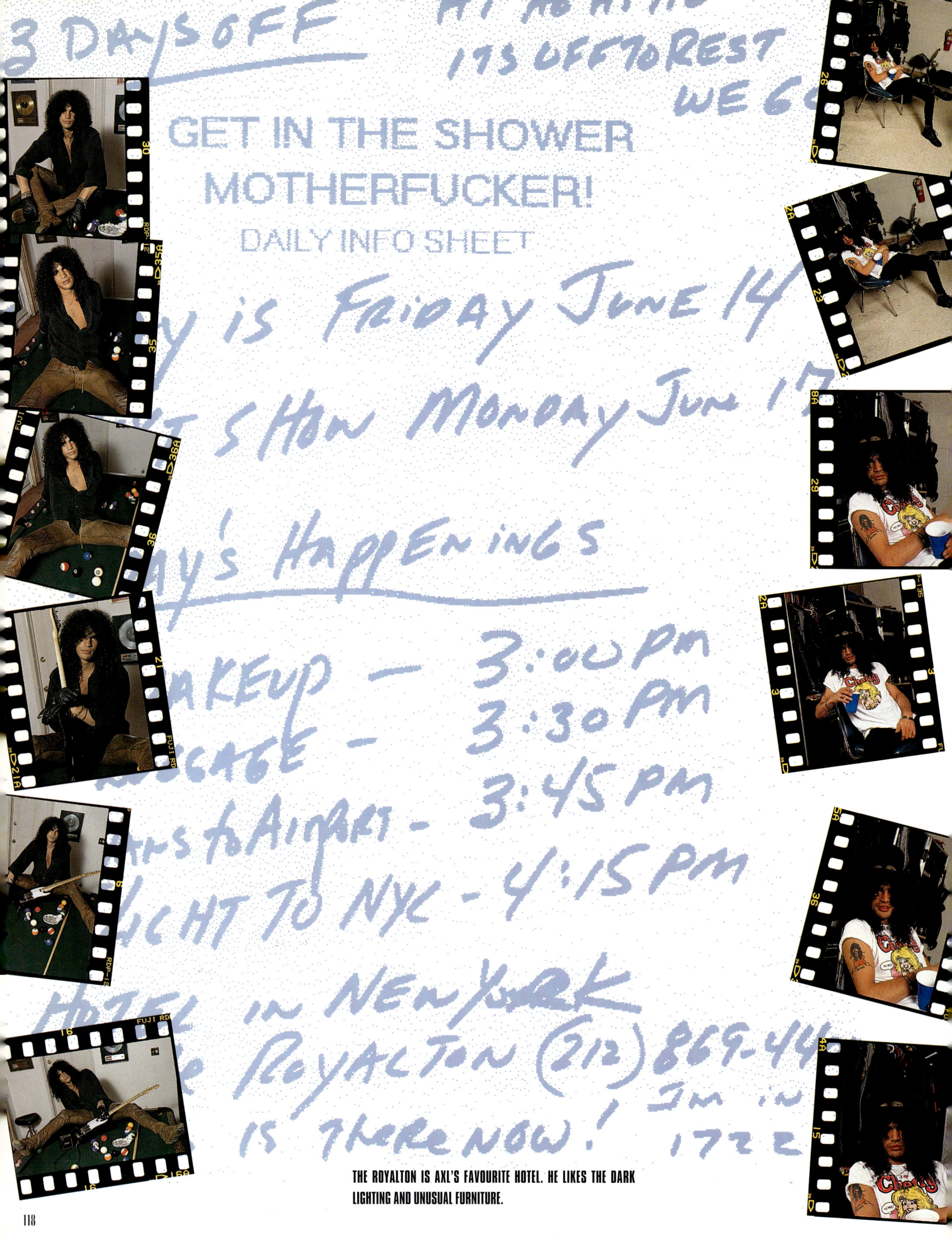



THE ROYALTON IS AXL'S FAVOURITE HOTEL. HE LIKES THE DARK LIGHTING AND UNUSUAL FURNITURE.

THE BACKSTAGE AREA WAS SEPARATED INTO THE BAND'S DRESSING ROOM AND AXL'S DRESSING ROOM. THE BAND ALWAYS HAD A MASSIVE STEREO AND TV IN A HUGE FLIGHT CASE WHICH STARTED PUMPING OUT MUSIC FROM THE MOMENT IT WAS UNPACKED, RIGHT UP TO WHEN THE BAND LEFT THE GIG.

IZZY NEVER TRAVELLED ON THE PLANE, EXCEPT ONCE. HE ALWAYS WENT FROM GIG TO GIG IN HIS OWN TOUR BUS WITH HIS WIFE AND DOG. IT WAS REFITTED TO INCLUDE A BEDROOM WITH A BED, BAR, KITCHEN, SHOWER, LOUNGE AND IN THE BAY, THERE WAS THE BIGGEST EVER SOUND SYSTEM SEEN ON FOUR WHEELS, COMPLETE WITH SATELLITE TV.

GN'R'S DRESSING ROOM TV WAS LINKED UP TO THE VIDEO CAMERAS FRONT STAGE SO THAT THE BAND COULD WATCH THE SUPPORT ACT. DURING THE INTERVAL, THE CAMERAS WOULD FOCUS ON THE AUDIENCE AND WORD GOT OUT THAT THE BAND WOULD BE WATCHING AND CHOOSING GIRLS FOR THE AFTER SHOW PARTY. THE REALLY DARING ONES WOULD GET ONTO SOMEONE'S SHOULDERS AND EXPOSE THEIR BOOBS FOR THE CAMERAS. WORD SPREAD, AND BY THE NEXT GIG, THIS HAPPENED AGAIN AND VERY SOON IT BECAME A REGULAR FEATURE AT EVERY SHOW.

THE BAND'S FAVOURITE TIPPLES ARE AS FOLLOWS:-

AXL     CHAMPAGNE AND WHITE WINE
SLASH     JAGERMEISTER, JACK AND COKE, AND BLACK DEATH VODKA
DUFF     VODKA AND CRANBERRY JUICE
MATT     BEER
IZZY     MINERAL WATER
DIZZY     JACK AND COKE, BEER

THE AFTER SHOW PARTIES WOULD SOMETIMES LAST UNTIL 4AM.



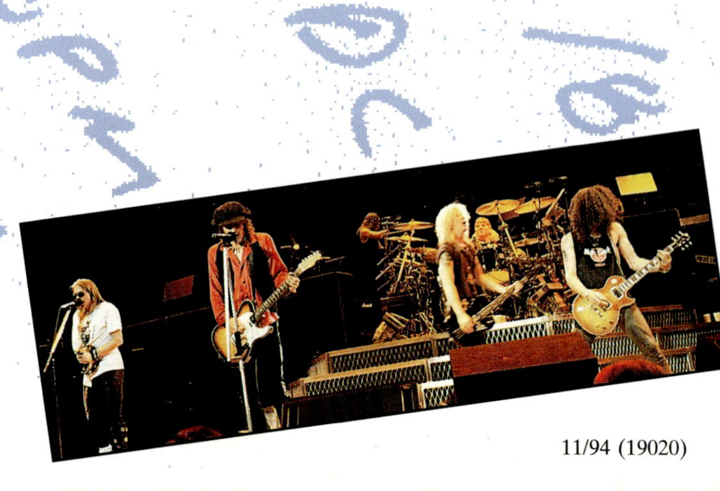